A FIGHTING *Chance*

Overcoming the Academic and Domestic Struggles of Children in Foster Care

DR. BRITTANY BUSH

T&J PUBLISHERS

A SMALL INDEPENDENT PUBLISHER WITH A BIG VOICE

Printed in the United States of America by
T&J Publishers (Atlanta, GA.)
www.TandJPublishers.com

Cover Design by Timothy Flemming, Jr. (T&J Publishers)
Book Format/Layout by Timothy Flemming, Jr.

ISBN: 978-1-7345105-0-8

To contact the author, send inquiries and requests to:
Email: BrittanyBush319@yahoo.com
Instagram: Inspiration319

Dedications

First, this book is dedicated to the thousands of children in the foster care system who struggle every day to beat the odds stacked against them. Their tenacity has inspired me in such a way that I have decided to dedicate my professional career attempting to improve their academic lives. This is an attempt at making others aware of the struggles foster children experience both academically and in the home. I hope to be the voice that ignites a change which gives these children A FIGHTING CHANCE at having a productive life; free from hurt, fear, uncertainty, and inconsistencies. I will forever be an advocate for children in foster care; providing a voice to the voiceless and bringing awareness to the issues they encounter.

Second, I want to thank my parents who made the necessary sacrifices to ensure that I was able to achieve my goals. My parents have always been my motivation to continue on, even when I felt like giving up. The hard work and determination they have displayed throughout my life and the constant sacrifices made for my brother and me, inspired me to achieve the most academically. Thus, igniting my passion for learning and ensuring that all children have the opportunity to receive the best education possible.

Lastly, my closest friends and colleagues have been the calm to the storms that arose during this process. I thank you for being my voice of reason when I wanted to quit. I thank you for allowing me to be who I am and for entertaining my passions. Thank you for always reassuring me when I doubted myself or was unsure of the vision. Thank you all for your unwavering love and support.

"Change will not come if we wait for some other person or some other time. We are the ones we've been waiting for. We are the change that we seek."

- Barack Obama

Table of Contents

was her job to assure that volunteer advocates were advocating appropriately and were using and aware of all possible resources. She was also responsible for ensuring that advocates were fulfilling their necessary requirements for continuing education and training. Moreover, Ms. Bush also served as the Development Coordinator for the organization--collaborating with community partners and helping to find opportunities to market our organization in terms of services and additional funding. After resigning from organization to pursue her passion for teaching, Ms. Bush continued to be an asset to the program by still agreeing to help train new advocates.

Dr. Brittany Bush is an Ambassador to all children. She not only educates the students she teaches, but she also consistently looks out for the well-being and betterment of all children to whom she sees a need. Dr. Bush has and continues to fight to help give children a fighting chance at being successful. Now her goal is to help others do the same by providing to the body of work regarding educating children in the system. Children in foster care are among the most vulnerable populations within the school system. Statistically speaking, the odds are stacked against them—socially, economically, and environmentally. These young people are sadly predisposed to disadvantage. During my time in child advocacy, it was evidenced that less than 12% of children in foster care would graduate from high school. This thought was alarming; especially with the number of resources and programs actually available to these children. Those reading this work are sure to be informed, intrigued, and inspired. Dr. Bush's research, as well as her personal and first-hand accounts and knowledge will draw readers into a greater understanding of what is needed to better provide educational support to students who have experienced or are experiencing various forms of abuse and neglect. Hopefully there will also be an increase in the readers empathy towards this population of youth, as well as increased emotional intelligence. Again, who better to expound on "a fighting chance" for than disadvantaged population than a true fighter for herself and others. Since I've known her, Dr. Bush has been the go-getter. This fact remains true, as she has beat me to the finish line in completing our doctoral studies. I by no means am jealous or envious. On the contrary, I am all the more inspired, and I am so proud to support and endorse this work. Congratulations Brittany!

Dawn Charleston-Green, M.Ed.
Veteran, U.S. Army
Minister and Faith, Youth & Family Advocate

Abstract

THE PURPOSE OF THE QUALITATIVE NARRATIVE INQUIRY study was to investigate the perceptions of Augusta, Richmond County teachers, school administrators, and counselors related to the home and academic supports children in the foster care system receive as well as the effects home and academic supports have on the students' academic experience. The general problem was children in the foster care system may not have the support needed to engage in a positive school experience.[84, 107] The specific problem was that in Richmond County there were approximately 3,000 open cases of children in the foster care system. At the end of the 2016 fiscal year, less than 11% of foster care students are projected to graduate from high school, highlighting the improvements needed to assist in closing the academic gaps for foster children (D.C. Gibson, personal communication, June 13, 2017). Richmond County teachers, school counselors, and administrators participated in an open-ended written narrative questionnaire. The responses were analyzed using thematic analysis, forming the major themes of meeting basic needs, caring and responsive foster parents, lack of communication, behavioral and emotional concerns, lack of student services, and training. Implications of the research findings indicated that children in the foster care system are getting basic needs met by foster parents; however, they are experiencing academic difficulties in school due to the students' placement instability, lack of supplemental therapeutic and academic interventions, as well as the absence of training for educators and other school officials.

Chapter One

Foster Care And The Educational System

EDUCATION LEVEL IS ONE OF THE LEADING predictors of success and failure in later life.[63] Research has indicated that there is a connection between dropouts, poverty, delinquency, financial struggles, and homelessness.[79] According to Neely and Griffin, key factors that are related to school dropouts include instability of home lives, teachers not taking responsibility for the classroom and showing interest in students passing or failing, and difficulties with academics; more specifically, understanding course material.[20, 79, 84] One subgroup of students who may experience many or all factors, especially instability of home lives, are children in the foster care system. Causing a great deal of academic suffering.[3, 20, 97]

According to the U.S. Department of Health and

Human Services, Administration for Children and Families, Administration on Children, Youth and Families, Children's Bureau (2016), by the end of July 2015, 415,129 entered the United States foster care system. According to the Georgia Division of Family and Children Services (2016), 11, 551 children entered the foster care system in the state of Georgia. 21% of children in the U.S. between 6 and 10 years of age are at risk of impeding future progress if developmental and academic interventions are not implemented at an elementary level.[3, 97] Foster children work below grade level, have a higher rate of absences and disciplinary referrals, and have been retained at least once during his or her academic career.[3, 107]

According to Zetlin, Weinberg, and Shea (2010), aside from attendance, other obstacles contribute to poor academic support and educational barriers such as: difficulty concentrating in the classroom, incomplete homework and class assignments, disorganization of school material, and emotional instability as it relates to birth parents, and lack of support from foster caretakers; leading to many foster care youth dropping out of school and experiencing a potential future of homelessness.[3, 107]

According to Rios and Rocco, foster youth report that many academic barriers were related to relationships with teachers, administrators, and counselors. Foster youth indicated that teachers are less interested in understanding foster care and the impact that it can have on academic progress. Teachers are not maintaining high expectations or rigorous curriculum, thus widening the academic gap. Counselors and administrators are not ensuring that foster youth are getting additional assistance for academic and emotional support needed to ensure success.[84]

The current study is important because it can bring awareness to the needs of foster students and the types of support needed. The study's findings could be used to further inform foster parents and school officials of the importance of maintaining a supportive home and academic environment; to insure foster care children are able to have a positive school experience. Chapter one will be a presentation of background knowledge as it relates to children, foster care, and teachers in the educational setting, an extension of the research problem, and the scope of the study. Further, assumptions and limitations will be discussed in detail followed by delimitations and theoretical framework.

BACKGROUND OF THE PROBLEM

Children in the foster care system can be removed from their homes and placed with alternate caregivers for reasons including neglect, physical, sexual, or emotional abuse. Foster children are subsequently placed with either a relative placement or an unfamiliar foster caregiver. In the early 1900s, the foster care system was constructed to mend adverse family conditions that may interfere with the physical, emotional, and mental development of children.[6] It is expected that foster care parents provide a supportive environment to offset the negativity experienced by the children in their home environment; while helping foster children learn life skills and gain a holistic domestic experience needed to assist in creating a positive future.[6, 84] There is a significant amount of research that indicated children growing up in the foster care system present with serious social, emotional, and behavioral problems.[3, 6, 20]

Foster caretakers are ideally temporary caregivers for children until the adverse conditions of the previous home environment are eliminated and the children are able to return home.[3] Realistically, all foster care circumstances do not fall within ideal parameters, and foster caretakers can become long term or permanent caregivers through the process of adoption or guardianship.[3, 6, 20] According to Salas, García-Martín, Fuentes, and Bernedo (2015), foster caretakers are made aware of the problems foster children may experience when placed in their homes; then, advised and encouraged to be patient, loving, and supportive throughout the foster child's transition. Many factors can influence the transition process. The age of the child was an imperative factor that had an immediate impact on the integration process of the foster child into foster families.[88] Younger children seem to have an easier time adjusting and integrating into a new environment, and many foster caretakers express a preference for younger children as opposed to older children. The temperament of the caretaker as well as the temperament of the child has a significant effect on the success of the foster care placement. Foster care workers are encouraged to assign foster care children to foster caregivers who demonstrate similar temperaments. Families who experience incongruence in temperaments may create the catalyst for a strained relationship.[88]

When domestic relationships are strained, the children may begin to act out in undesirable ways; such as physical, emotional, or sexual outburst. During these instances, foster caretakers express an increased amount of stress and feel overly burdened with the responsibility of caring for the child.[6, 84] Increased stress and burden could lead to reduced domestic support from the caregiver to the child, or a disruption in placement; negatively impacting the child's life experiences.[88] Behavioral and supportive concerns not only show evident in the home lives of foster children, but can also extend into educational experiences.[79]

According to Tyre (2012), teachers of students in the foster care system often complain about not having knowledge of the child being placed in foster care; therefore, not being provided with the resources to intervene academically and attend to his or her unique needs.[32] When teachers are made aware of the domestic status of children (i.e. being in a foster care placement) they do not feel supported by other agencies involved with the child: including, foster care workers and foster caretakers.[32] Further, students report not having necessary resources or caring faculty and staff members to help them excel academically.[84]

PROBLEM STATEMENT

Children in the foster care system may not have the support needed to engage in a positive school experience.[84, 107] Academically, foster care students are more likely than their peers to perform below grade level and are less likely to graduate from high school.[20, 79, 84] This may be due to the transient nature of foster care students, transitioning from placement to placement and the instability it causes within the lives of these students.[6, 79]

Students in the foster care system have been identified as having increased behavior referrals, concerns with attendance, and lack of family support.[6] Because 21 percent of the United States foster care population will be unsuccessful in school at an elementary level, and 75% of all foster care children are working below grade level, it is imperative to find interventions at an early stage to assist in the academic advancement of foster care students to help them lead a more successful and prosperous future.[97] While the need for early intervention has been identified for foster care students, educators report not having proper training and resources needed to help foster care students become academically successful.[32]

Specifically that in Georgia there were approximately 8,000 children in the foster care system. In Augusta, Richmond County there were approximately 3,000 open cases of children in the foster care system at the end of the 2016 fiscal year (D.C. Gibson, personal communication, June 13, 2017). According to D. C. Gibson (personal communication, June 13, 2017) the graduation rate for children in the foster care system is between 8% and 11%. This data is directly related to the improvements needed to help close the academic gaps experienced by this subgroup of students; thus, increasing the likelihood they will enter into post-secondary education. In examining all of the facets related to the academic success of foster care children, one must not only consider the foster child, but his or her caretakers and teachers. Children in the foster care system may not have the support needed from foster caretakers or school officials to engage in a positive school experience. The aforementioned information demonstrates a need for a study designed to explore the supports that foster care children receive from foster caretakers and academic environments that influence school experience.

PURPOSE OF STUDY

The purpose of the study was to explore the academic and home supports foster care children received that could potentially influence school experiences (Craig, Zou, & Poimbeauf, 2014). The current study targeted 33 elementary schools with a population of foster care students. The researcher collaborated with the Richmond County Board of Education to obtain information to conduct research in its schools. The problem was addressed by requesting the responses of teachers, administrators, and counselors of students who have been in the foster care system. Perceptions of the support foster children were receiving from foster caretakers and the school environment was gathered using a narrative questionnaire concerning academic concerns and overall perception of school experience and home support of foster care students. The intent of this study was to explore those perceptions of each participant and address weaknesses in academic and home support; providing possible methods or techniques to aid in the enhancement of student achievement.

POPULATION AND SAMPLE

The population identified consisted of teachers, administrators, and school counselors in the 33 elementary schools in the Augusta, Richmond County school district. The total number of elementary teachers in Richmond County was 757. There were 70 elementary administrators, and 33 elementary school counselors. The total population of potential participants was 860. In the current study, the researcher was interested in teachers, administrators, and counselors who have had a minimum of two years of personal experience with children in the foster care system. To obtain a meaningful sample, the researcher conducted a purposeful sample, obtaining 24 substantial responses.[80] A purposeful sample was selected because the researcher had the ability to identify individuals who were able to provide the most meaningful information regarding the topic of interest. Specifically, elementary teachers, administrators, and counselors in Augusta, Richmond County.

SIGNIFICANCE OF THE STUDY

Addressing academic pitfalls at the elementary school level and implementing appropriate interventions to increase the probability of academic success can help close the academic gap.[84] Identifying and understanding barriers at an elementary level could be used to formulate interventions or preventative measures designed to enhance academic progress throughout middle and high school levels.[63,79] Providing school officials with constructive intervention methods and foster care providers with necessary knowledge regarding the significance of domestic support, administrators are able to implement trainings for teachers and academic personnel making them more equipped to educate students in foster care.[32] Educational leaders will then be able to apply for additional funding for external resources identified as beneficial to the academic success of the foster care student population.

Because foster care takers are provided compensation through government funding, it is imperative that the care provided is appropriate and supportive.[32] Previous literature has examined the foster care student population and the obstacles that are associated with instability and lack of educational and family support.[18] However, little research has been conducted on expressing the needs of this population and even less on interventions that can assist in closing the educational gap.[97] By conducting the qualitative narrative inquiry study, significant information may arise from understanding the participants' experience and essential components that encompass the identified experience.[24]

SIGNIFICANCE OF THE STUDY TO EDUCATIONAL LEADERSHIP

If it is identified that lack of support from educators is negatively affecting foster care student's positive school experience, the insight gained from the current study could aid and encourage educational leaders to engage in early intervention measures; addressing academic concerns in the classroom. Tackling concerns at an early stage proves beneficial because research has indicated that the longer a child struggles academically in school, the more likely he or she will drop out; being subjected to a future of homelessness.[63] Plainly stated, findings from the current study could ultimately lead to a theory on issues that may need to be addressed beforehand to help increase the academic performance of foster care students, decreasing the chance of dropouts.[79]

The findings can be used as the foundation or rationale for potential professional development courses offered to educators and educational leaders. Providing the necessary tools to create a nurturing academic environment and the most appropriate way to handle children in the care of a foster caretaker.[6, 79] Educational leaders can collaborate with school counselors and social workers to formulate support groups for foster caretakers aimed to provide an outlet for caretakers to express concerns in a safe environment. Foster caretakers will also have the opportunity to receive supplemental training on the importance of domestic support and the effects it has on the emotional and academic development of children (Garcia et al., 2015).[49] Lastly, the findings of this study may express a need for support groups for children in the foster care system. Having a safe environment of like peers may help foster students cope with difficulties of being in the foster care system.[32, 107] The counselors or trained leaders of the support group will also be able to provide students with coping strategies to deal with the emotional strains that come with being placed in foster care and academic interventions to compensate for the lack of domestic support if that is identified as a primary issue.[97]

CONCEPTUAL FRAMEWORK

In an attempt to understand the emotional and physiological needs of foster care students, one must first understand the conceptual framework surrounding the basis for unfulfilled needs of children in the foster care system.[51] One of the most profound theories that set the backdrop in understanding what students in the foster care system go through is Maslow's theory of Hierarchy of Needs. According to the theorist Maslow (1943), a hierarchy of needs exists that governs an individual's quality of life. At the beginning level of the hierarchy are the physiological needs of food, clothing, and shelter. If physiological needs are not met, then the individual is not able to progress through the subsequent levels of the hierarchy.[67] For example, if an individual is hungry, or is concerned with not having clothing or shelter, he or she must satisfy those immediate needs before being able to transcend to the next level in the Hierarchy of Needs, safety and security.

Often times, in situations where children are removed from homes, it is due to inadequate food, clothing, and shelter. In addition, considering the transient nature of foster children, they are taken out of their familiar domestic environment and placed in an unfamiliar setting. One can consider the living situation of a foster care child to be unstable or unfulfilled. Based on the founding principles of Maslow's Hierarchy of Needs, children in the foster care system have most basic needs interrupted or dismantled. As indicated by Maslow, until children in the foster care system have basic needs restored by those individuals identified by the legal system to provide a supplemental stable and loving environment, children in the foster care system will not be able to progress to the next level in the hierarchy. Maslow went on to argue in the 1943 article, if needs are not met and the individual is plagued by physiological needs, all other subsequent needs are eliminated. Plainly stated, if an individual is hungry or lacking shelter, he or she will be unable to properly function until those basic needs are met.

Once an individual has satisfied basic needs of food, clothing, shelter, water, and air, their focus then becomes establishing safety and security within themselves and the environment. According to Maslow, an adult's need for safety is not as immediate and obvious as that of a child or infant. Maslow indicated that children demonstrate feelings of being unsafe in diverse ways, such as being startled by loud or sudden noises and crying when facing fear or feelings of discomfort. Children may demonstrate feelings of fear through illness or pain. They may complain of headaches and stomachaches or may vomit uncontrollably.[67]

Children and infants may experience threats to feelings of safety and security in the presence of unfamiliar stimuli, unorganized situations, and unstructured environments.[67] This is evident when foster care children are sometimes placed with unfamiliar caretakers and primary caregivers can change periodically; causing children to lack the feeling of comfort and security in their living environment. Because of the child's desire to maintain a sense of safety and security, Maslow suggested that children may cling to his or her parent or caregiver as a testament of the importance of the feeling of safety. Children seek security from the adults in their lives and if that relationship is threatened or nonexistent, the desire for safety and security is amplified and the child is unable to progress through Maslow's hierarchy until the need is satisfied.

An additional theory that can be used to conceptualize emotional benefits of family support is the Bowen family systems theory. The Bowen family systems theory indicated that humans are emotionally connected to families. Within the family unit, the emotions and actions of one person is interdependent on another.[64, 66] Family members seek the approval and support of other family members and react to the needs, expectations, and disappointments of others. This emotional interdependence can be both a positive and negative aspect. In the positive realm, family members use interdependence to create an intimate bond that promotes unity, protection, and a sense of responsibility. On the other hand, the negative aspects to emotional interdependence when family members become anxious, angry, or depressed, the connectedness causes other members to experience those same feelings.[64, 66] Consequently, this could lead to isolation and behavior concerns.

According to Knauth (2003), while family members are somewhat emotionally connected, there should exist a differentiation of self; meaning that one has the ability to separate his or her emotional system from one's intellectual systems. In poorly differentiated families, communication is poor and secrets exist. Holding on to secrets can cause emotional, intellectual, and physical illnesses or frustration.[64] For children in the foster care system who do not have constant communication with their biological parents or family members, there may exists a buildup of secrets; causing anxiety, frustration, and depression from the unknown.[64, 66] These negative feelings could ultimately hinder their intellectual processing.[64] If children in the foster care system are not able to build domestic relationships and open lines of communication with alternative support systems, they may not be able to develop a healthy differentiation of self.[64, 66]

To further conceptualize the emotional and physiological needs of foster care students, Bowlby's attachment theory proved influential in understanding the desire and need for attachment in children.[97, 101] Bowlby's attachment theory stated children are born into this world with an innate desire to bond or form attachments. Attachments provide nurturing support and are also necessary for survival.[97] Infants long for the desire to be in close proximity to familiar individuals. When that proximity is threatened, infants engage in what Bowlby calls social releasers. Social releasers are things that infants do to gain the attention of the caregiver. For example: crying, cooing, and smiling.[97, 101]

According to Vicedo, Bowlby indicated that in order for children to maintain a healthy psychological state and future endeavors, they must maintain a solid nuclear family. If anything causes a threat or harm to the family foundation, it can be detrimental and depriving for children. Considering the findings of Bowlby, children in the foster care system have suffered several threats to the nuclear family. Some children only suffer the loss of proximity, meaning the parent is no longer there on a daily basis; while others suffer abuse and neglect, which threatens the parent-child relationship, causing undue harm.[6, 101] Bowlby's attachment theory would indicate that because of these factors, children in the foster care system will suffer from psychological stressors and a potential future of delinquency.[101]

Chapter Two

Review of the Literature

UNDERSTANDING THE CHALLENGES FOSTER CARE children may face both academically and domestically, may provide social workers, foster care organizations, and school officials with information needed to enhance academic experience. Chapter 2 presents a review of historical and current literature regarding foster care and academics, the benefits of home support, and the challenges faced by children in the foster care system. Chapter 2 also provides the conceptual framework including an in-depth review of Maslow's Hierarchy of Needs, Bowlby's Attachment Theory, and Bowen's Family Systems Theory. All theories are associated with the concepts of basic needs, the benefits of support systems, and available resources.

A comprehensive review of previous and current literature, demonstrated an interest in the foster care student population and the challenges associated with their instability and lack of educational and family support.[6, 18, 79] However, little research has been conducted on expressing the needs of this population based upon the perceptions of school officials and even less on interventions that can assist in closing the educational gap at an elementary level.[97] By conducting this qualitative narrative inquiry study, momentous findings may surface contributing to this gap in the literature.

HISTORICAL CONTENT

The evolution of child protective services in the United States has evolved over the decades. During the seventeenth and eighteenth century Europe, there were no set of laws that directly related to the welfare of children.[41, 50, 60, 95] Instead, there were a series of community laws that protected children in the orphanage and the children of the poor.[95] This population of children was targeted by the community because children over the age of four were considered an asset to the household. Additional attention was given to children of the poor, because the community felt a responsibility to rid the bad behaviors potentially learned from their parents.[50] Instead, they desired to have the children become a respected member of society.[41, 50] These social provisions originated from the English Poor Law tradition. According to the English Poor Law tradition, there were four ways in which children in need of community intervention were handled. The goal of all four options was to ensure the best interest of the community and not the children.[41, 50, 60, 95]

The first option was known as outdoor relief. Outdoor relief consisted of the community providing the family with a small allocation to sustain their home. The second option was called farming-out. This system auctioned individuals who were considered poor, to citizens who agreed to house them with their families for a previously agreed upon fee. Almshouse or poorhouses were considered the third option for impoverished children and adults; these homes were public institutions designed to care for underprivileged children and adults. The fourth option to be considered was a plan to release children to households where they would be cared for or taught a trade. The children repaid the families by showing respect for generosity and providing labor until the debt was paid in full. The latter option was known as indentured.[41, 50, 60, 95]

During the nineteenth century, several contributing factors shaped the economic status and child welfare laws of the United States. With the implementation of slavery in the U.S., the need for indentured white children decreased. There was also a division of class where the labor of children and women were no longer required and families could focus more on the educational and developmental needs of children. On the other hand, the end of the Civil War brought several immigrant families and impoverished children to the United States.[41, 50, 60, 95] This factor led to the increase in orphanages.[50] Because several reporters were publically opposed to the use of outdoor relief, farming-out, and indentured methods of dealing with impoverished and special needs children due to inhumane and maltreatment, the use of orphanages and almshouses increased.[50, 60, 95] However, there were no public laws prohibiting the care of children.[41, 50, 60, 95]

With the increased public knowledge of the ill conditions of almshouses, the Children's Aid Society was established in New York. Hundreds of foster care homes were established under the Social Aid Society, designed to provide children with Christians home with moral training. While in the protestant sector, Children's Home Society was established to provide free foster homes. While the free foster homes aided in filling a need, there were extensive criticisms. One of the main critiques was that children living in the home were expected to pay for food and bed through labor. Children were also being mistreated and exposed to immoral influences. Additionally, concern was raised that foster families did not receive the necessary resources to educate the students in their homes, nor did they possess the Roman Catholic religious training to ensure that the children maintained a solid religious foundation.[41, 50, 60, 95]

During the end of the nineteenth century, community members became increasingly concerned about the chances of dependent children becoming delinquent ad lacking the proper education needed become an active member of society. The historical case of Mary Ellen was the catalyst that brought attention to the welfare of children and the obligations of families to ensure the basic needs of children are met.[41, 50, 60, 95] Mary Ellen's story began when a neighbor was concerned about the abusive treatment Mary Ellen was receiving from her caretakers.[50, 57, 60, 95] The neighbor sought help from child welfare institutions but were not able to provide assistance. The neighbor then sought the assistance of Henry Bergh, the president of the Society for the Prevention of Cruelty to Animals (SPCA), who later took the case to court. Henry Bergh requested that Mary Ellen be removed from her home immediately. The results of the court hearing made it apparent that laws needed to be put in place to protect the welfare of children as it relates to cruelty and maltreatment.[50, 57, 60, 95] Several organizations sought to aid in the protection of children, with one of more immediate implementations being friendly visitors.[50]

Friendly visitors were runners who made visits to the homes of impoverished homes. The visitors would assess the needs of families and implement resources where deemed necessary to improve their way of living.[50] If children were not able to be cared for by their families, then they were sent to live with private families. With the abolishment of almshouse each state developed individual state programs for private homes. This marked the beginning of the twentieth century when federal regulations were being placed on the welfare of children.[41, 50, 60, 95]

FOSTER CAREGIVERS AND PLACEMENTS

Children are placed into the foster care system due to abuse or neglect in current living situations. If it is identified that the child(ren) is not able to stay in the home, they can be displaced to another relative, group facility, or non-relative foster caregiver. The government's involvement in the lives of families is not meant to be a permanent situation.[2, 96] Ideally, foster care placement is intended to be a temporary placement until a stable placement is located to permanently care for the child(ren). Permanent placement can either be with their current foster caregiver through adoption, or transfer of custody or guardianship to alternate caregiver. Likewise, permanency of placement can be achieved outside of the current foster placement through emancipation, or reunification with original caregiver. While a child's stay in the foster care system is preferably temporary, it is contingent upon several independent factors.[2, 96]

FOSTER CAREGIVERS

Often times, foster parents are trained and supervised by foster care agencies responsible for the foster parent and the children placed in their homes. While foster care agencies are designed to offer support and resources to foster parents, many foster caregivers indicated they do not feel they were provided adequate information or resources. Foster parents have indicated that they do not feel trusted or valued by the social services caseworkers, and when there is a need for additional time and support for a troubled child, the caseworker is often unavailable. This in return causes a great deal of stress and strain on the relationship between the foster parent and the caseworker.[13, 14, 15, 82]

Legally, in order for foster parents to accept children into their home, the Foster Care Independence Act of 1999 indicated that foster parents must undergo training prior to placement. However, the guidelines for training are not specific and are left for interpretation by individual agencies.[15] Likewise, the requirement for continuous in-service trainings is common, but the frequency and number of hours varies across agencies as well.[13, 14, 15] In terms of specialized training for therapeutic/treatment foster caregivers, there is no statewide concusses. Therapeutic or treatment foster caregivers are specialized in caring for children with special mental, physical, or behavioral needs. While in some states it is a requirement for these unique set of foster parents to undergo additional, specialized training, it is not commonplace across the nation.[13, 15]

When foster parents were asked for perceptions regarding the deficits in foster care placement agencies, foster parents indicate a need for additional and specialized training. Specialized training would include obtaining knowledge and resources for children who are classified as having special medical or mental health needs.[13, 14, 15, 82] According to Brown (2008), foster parents who undergo specific and multifaceted training have a greater success rate with children placed in their homes. They have also been identified as taking longer to burn out and report being much more satisfied with the fostering process and the agency.[13, 14, 15, 82] Additional deficits highlighted by foster parents included: Being able to have access to more detailed information about the child being placed in their home provide foster parents and children an opportunity to be better matched by personality and temperament. Having a clear understanding of the roles and expectations of a foster parent.[13, 15] Ideally, foster parents have indicated, that if all of the previously stated concerns are met, then foster children placed in their care will have a more successful stay.[13, 14, 15, 82]

LENGTH OF TIME IN FOSTER CARE

One of the major factors that can contribute to the time it takes a child to obtain a stable placement in the foster care system is the parent's ability to care for them and provide a suitable and stable placement so that the children may return home.[16, 58, 103] Another aspect that is directly related to the foster child and the foster caregiver is the disruption of placement. A disruption of placement occurs when there is some sort of tension between the child and the foster caregiver (relative or non-relative). Disruptions in placement can be due to mismatched personality traits by the foster care giver and the child. The temperaments of both may be so drastically different, that it causes a great amount of conflict in the home.[16, 58, 103]

Additionally, foster care givers may have unrealistic expectations of the foster child entering into their home and the frustration between both parties can cause a build-up of tension. On the other hand, a foster child may simply have several behavioral related issues, causing various contributing factors including: Emotional distress from being separated from primary caregivers and the uncertainty of reunification, misplaced anger due to the emotional and psychological strains of the situation, and unresolved mental health needs. Children who experience several placement moves are subject to a greater severity of behavior and emotional problems, are less likely to find a permanent placement, and spend more time in the foster care system. Further, disruptions of placements accrue several financial expenses for the child welfare system. For this reason, unplanned placement moves are regulated by the federal government. Social workers must notify court officials of any planned and unplanned moves.[16, 58, 103]

LAWS REGARDING CHANGE IN PLACEMENT

A change in placement can also mean a change in schools and friends, thereby disrupting familiar bonds that may have existed in this academic setting. [16, 58, 103] Because of this, the federal government has laws in place to help prevent students in the foster care system from having to change schools when moving placements. During the 2002 reauthorization of the McKinney-Vento Act, a sector of No Child Left Behind, the definition of a "homeless student" was clearly defined which included children in the foster care system.[53, 72] According to the McKinney-Vento Act, children who are classified as being homeless are given special considerations when it comes to education. Specifically, students classified as homeless should be given an opportunity to remain in their original zoned school or school of last enrollment, even if a change placement occurs. The school district and social service providers should collaborate on a plan that offers educational stability and continued transportation to school.[53, 72] Theoretically, the McKinney-Vento Act seems plausible; however, realistically putting the plan into action can be difficult.

While the law states that transportation should be provided to those students who have a desire to attend the same school, it does not mandate who is responsible for arranging transportation.[53, 72] The law also indicates that if it becomes unfeasible for the child to remain in the previous school, social service providers have the option to change schools. If foster caregivers are not in a position or willing to travel an extended distance to transport the child to school, he or she may still be subject to a school change.[53, 72]

FOSTER CHILDREN AND ACADEMICS

Meese (2012) indicated that school age children respond to being in foster care differently depending upon age. Younger, elementary aged children are beginning to grasp the concept of being away from home, but they do not fully understand everything.[70] It is important for teachers to understand the developmental needs of foster students and respond in a more sensitive manner.[70] According to Meese, teachers have the ability to build meaningful relationships with students in the foster care system, by acknowledging their feelings and reassuring them that their feelings are normal.

EMOTIONAL AND MENTAL IMPLICATIONS

Children in foster care appear to lack progression of behavioral and emotional development during their time in care. This could be due to stress related to begin removed from home or the maltreatment endured while residing in the home. In addition to the maltreatment suffered by children entering foster care, educational neglect is also common in negligent households.[39, 47, 89, 91] Further, the instability of foster care placements and changes in schools and educators, disrupts any improvements to education.[89, 107, 108] Actually, children in foster care systems have been identified as having increased behavioral concerns leading to an augmented number of suspensions or expulsions. Children in the foster care system are also more likely to be retained in a grade due to an increased number of abscesses or failure to meet academic requirements.[89, 107, 108] An excessive number of children in the foster care system are determined to qualify for special education services.[89, 100, 106] Researchers theorized that this may be due to gaps in education caused by the transient nature of foster care students. There is concern that foster children are not being correctly identified for special education programs, thus being served inappropriately. A more appropriate remediation process may include specific interventions in the general education setting.[89, 100]

Research indicated that children in the foster care system suffer from both externalizing and internalizing problems. Externalizing problems are those problems that can be seen such as deliberately breaking rules and engaging in aggressive or delinquent behavior. Internalizing problems are those issues that are less visible such as anxiety, depressions, or somatic systems.[4, 61, 70] According to Berendo (2012), teachers report an increase in externalizing behaviors for children in the foster care system; causing disruption to the classroom setting. Berendo suggested that teachers may not notice the internalizing behaviors because in essence they are not disruptive. However, the way in which teachers responds to this population of children can make a drastic difference in how they react.[70]

FUTURE IMPLICATIONS

Aside from the more immediate concerns, academic struggles for children in the foster care system have future implications as well.[97, 100, 106] Children in the foster care system report lack of support in the home environment, such as having someone to help with homework or offer motivation. The difficulties foster care children face in school decreases chances of completing high school and attending post-secondary school. Those children who never obtain stability in living situations or furthering education will ultimately be removed from the foster care system and are subject to a life of homelessness.[97, 100, 106]

ACADEMIC RECOMMENDATIONS

It is recommended that in order for foster children to increase academic performance and work on closing the achievement gap, the children must stay in school as long as possible.[23, 100] This means the more a child moves schools, the less likely they are to progress academically. Instead of removing foster students from the general educational setting, Vacca (2008) suggested that students should stay with higher achieving peers and given the opportunity to succeed in challenging classes. Teachers should give more attention to those students and seek opportunities to find adult mentors to aid in building positive relationships. Educators and school administrators should increase communication between schools and welfare services, thus appointing someone to act as a strong educational advocate for foster care students.[23, 100]

CURRENT CONTENT

Foster caregivers and placements. Children enter into the foster care system for various reasons including: physical, mental, or verbal abuse by a parent or caregiver, neglect which could include unmet physical, medical or educational needs, or involvement in an abusive household. Once a report has been made to the Department of Family and Children Services, a proper investigation must be conducted in order to substantiate the need for government intervention. If the current placement is considered harmful and unsuitable for the children in the care of the parent or caregiver, they are removed and placed in an alternative placement. This placement can be with a willing and able relative or a state certified foster caregiver.[3, 6]

CONCERNS WITH FOSTER CARE PLACEMENTS

While children who enter foster care are removed from homes of maltreatment and abuse, there are several foster children who report experiencing maltreatment in the foster home. Most would believe that because all foster homes are thoroughly vetted by child protective services children would be in a safe environment; however, many reports have indicated ongoing abuse.[74] A large number of children entering the foster care system experience emotional, behavioral, and mental health issues. When children present with these concerns, it is important that caretakers have proper training to provide interventions or best practices when faced with trauma. Foster caretakers have stated that they did not have enough training on the special needs of foster children. Foster mothers reported experiencing elevated stress levels and negative interactions with children due to stress levels.[52, 86, 87]

Child welfare services have attempted to address the need by creating specialized therapeutic foster homes, where foster caretakers have special training to care for children who are classified as having emotional, behavioral, or mental health needs. Foster caretakers are required to take pre and in-service training classes to continuously increase knowledge and decrease negative behaviors in their homes. Other stressors and strain experienced in a foster care placement can be due to differences in temperament and parenting styles. If the parenting and disciplines styles of the foster caretaker is drastically different from that of the primary/biological caregivers, there could exists friction and resistance.[52, 86, 87]

PERCEPTIONS OF FOSTER CHILDREN

When considering the perceptions of the children in foster care, it was discussed that foster children felt a great deal of anxiety and resentment when suddenly placed into a foster home. Foster children indicated feeling unhappy with placements for fear that foster caretaker would not take adequate care of them. They expressed a need to feel included in the decision making process and stated that if they had prior knowledge before being moved, it would make the process less turmoil.[48] Children in the foster care system not only express a need to be involved in the placement process, but also in the goal setting process. Foster children indicated they prefer to be placed in homes that are close to where their family is located and feel more comfortable if they are able to maintain contact with biological parents.[17, 73] In order for foster placements to be successful, foster children must feel welcome in the foster parent's home and be supportive of school and extra-curricular activities.[73] Children in the foster care system who reported better relationships with foster care givers, reported a more positive experience in foster care along with higher self-esteem.[17]

IMPLICATIONS OF PLACEMENT CHANGES

Children in the foster system who undergo multiple placement changes face serious issues and setbacks.[52, 86, 87, 102] Factors that contribute to increased placement change include children with behavioral problems, mental health concerns, poor adaptability, and older children. Foster care children who undergo several unplanned moves are also subject to several school changes. Uprooting children from familiar schools not only dismantles established friendships, but it also causes gaps in learning. Students who move frequently are often unable to perform well academically, and experience symptoms of anxiety and depression.[52, 86, 87, 102]

FOSTER CHILDREN AND ACADEMICS

As previous research has indicated, children in the foster care system undergo a series of academic barriers. One of the most common barriers that hinder children from performing well academically are the mental obstacles present due to emotional baggage. Foster children undergo a great deal of stress when being separated from home and placed in unfamiliar territory. Foster children are categorized as having elevated levels of anxiety and depression, making it challenging for students to perform well in school.[42, 43, 44, 74, 75] Emotional distress can also be due to the abuse or neglect suffered at the hands of the original caregivers. According to Morton (2015), children who undergo several years of abuse can undergo feelings of disempowerment and anger. Children who have been abused are reluctant to speak and may become fearful of adults. They may feel worthless and shy away from engaging with others. On the other hand, feelings of anger may surface causing aggressive and delinquent behaviors in foster children.[74, 75] Children may also become defiant towards adults or authority figures. These factors are more prevalent in children who are placed with non-relative caregivers, than those who are placed with relatives.[43]

The behaviors expressed and experienced by foster children may transition into the academic sector. Foster children who experience feelings of anger may act out, causing several behavioral referrals. Foster care students, who spend a lot of time suspended or expelled, miss a great deal of information being taught in school. Frequent absences hinder academic progression and increases gaps in academic achievement. The wider the achievement gap for children in foster care, the less likely they are to remain in their appropriate grade.[42, 43, 74, 75] Plainly stated, the wider the gap between where foster care students should be academically and where they actually are, the more likely he or she will be retained in their current grade. Further, if the achievement gap becomes too large, students may then be referred for special education testing and services. Students who face several difficulties in school are less likely to graduate. Students who fail to obtain a stable education face a higher risk of homelessness.[74, 75]

ACADEMIC INTERVENTIONS

To assist the foster care population in making academic progression, research has suggested interventions that may increase achievement and academic skills.[22, 42] Implementing tutoring interventions has been shown to improve student achievement.[22, 42, 44] Tutoring can be conducted in the school, by an independent agency, or by a willing foster caretakers.[22, 44] Tutoring not only increases academic skill, but it can also increase self-esteem and motivation. Further, if the tutoring is conducted via foster caretaker, it may enhance the bond between the foster child and the caretaker. The foster child feels as though the caretaker is expressing an interest in their wellbeing, thus building relationships and formulating trust. Likewise, it is important for the caregiver to implement reasonable expectations. Caregiver expectations have been shown to have a positive influence on academic outcomes.[22, 42, 44]

FUTURE IMPLICATIONS

Children in the foster care system who do not perform well academically run the risk of negative future implications.

Re-entry into foster care and long stents in the foster care system, is a significant predictor of increased academic concerns for foster children. Children in foster care, who experience academic struggles, may not progress through grade school without retentions or special education services. Research has indicated that children who experience these difficulties run the risk of dropping out of school. Students who do not have a solid educational foundation are less likely to attend post-secondary institutions and may encounter a future of homelessness and poverty. Additionally, lack of a firm scholastic underpinning correlates with increased unplanned pregnancies to parents without adequate resources; leading to a new generation of children in the foster care system.[62, 84]

A FIGHTING CHANCE

Chapter Three

Conclusions And Recommendations

THE FINDINGS OF THIS STUDY SOUGHT TO PROVIDE insight into the perceived general problem that children in the foster care system may not have the support they need to engage in a positive school experience.[84, 107] Foster care students are more likely than their peers to perform below grade level and are less likely to graduate from high school, causing an increase rate of homelessness and poverty.[20, 79, 84] Children in the foster care system also have an elevated number of behavior referrals and truancy concerns.[20, 79]

Thematic analysis was used to identify major and subthemes that emerged from the data. The themes that were identified were basic needs met, caring and responsive foster parents, lack of communication, behavioral and emotional concerns, lack of student services, and training. Chapter three will include a summary of the study's findings and the correlation of the findings to each research question. Chapter three consists of implications of the findings and relevance to the literature, as well as the implications of the study to the theoretical framework. Chapter three concludes with an explanation of study limitations, and recommendations for leadership and future research.

FINDINGS OF STUDY

The researcher developed two research questions to help guide this study.

Research question one: The initial research question sought to explore the lived experiences of teachers, administrators, and school counselors as it relates to the domestic support children in the foster care system receives and the influence it may have on academic experiences. The responses from participants displayed evidence indicating that foster parents provide the basic needs (food, clothing, and shelter) for the foster children in their care. The participants' responses also indicated that foster parents are predominantly caring and responsive to the foster children. Subthemes suggested that foster parents tend to provide more to those foster children who they have for an extended amount of time or plan on adopting.

However, while there was an overwhelming number of references made by participants regarding foster parents being caring and responsive, some participants also made reference to the opposite; foster parents only providing the bare minimum of care, and providing poor quality of care to the foster children in their homes. While these references were not as frequent as those portraying foster parents in a positive light, this information is worth mentioning because it provides insight into the differences in dynamics that might exist in the homes of foster caretakers. The study's participants also made reference to another theme regarding the lack of communication between school officials and the foster parents. Some participants made reference to the foster parents inability to be physically present at the school due to other obligations. This may be a contributing factor as to why the communication between the two parties is limited.

Research question two: The second research question examined the perceptions of teachers, administrators, and counselors of elementary foster care students regarding the school's support systems and resources that may influence the student's academic experience. Three major themes were identified from the qualitative data acquired from the 19 participants. The most significant theme that emerged was the behavioral and emotional concerns displayed by foster children. The participants expressed that many foster parents have a limited ability to discipline and the instability of the home life for the children in foster care creates emotional and behavioral turmoil within these students causing a poor academic experience.

Participants further explained how academically behind students in the foster care system are, mainly due to their instability and frequent transitions and movements. From this, the second theme emerged regarding lack of services for this population of students to address the emotional, behavioral, and academic issues. The research participants conveyed they were not aware of any additional services provided and many of the students were in need of academic and therapeutic services in the school system, but were not receiving them. The third major theme associated with the second research question was lack of training for teachers, counselors, and administrators in working with children in the foster care system. Some participants expressed that a training of this nature would be helpful, but it was not currently being offered. On the other hand, other participants who indicated that they had received training, did so through previous employers or academic degree programs.

IMPLICATION OF STUDY FINDINGS AND PARALLELS TO LITERATURE

A significant amount of research was conducted exploring the relationships between foster children and foster caregivers.[74] While the research highlights the strains that may exist between the two, the themes that emerged from the narrative responses does not solely support this. The majority of participants express that foster parents provide a caring environment for the children in their care, providing the basic needs of food, clothing, and shelter. While there are some indications of poor quality of care by some foster parents, the references of caring and attentive foster parents outweigh the negative experiences. With that being said, it appears that the foster children referenced in the current data are receiving the support needed in the homes by the foster parents responsible for caring for them.

ACADEMIC SUPPORT

The research indicates that students in the foster care system experience difficulties in school including increased behavioral referrals and gaps in their academic achievement. Students in the foster care system are less likely to attend post-secondary school, more likely to be retained, or unnecessarily placed in special education programs, and may ultimately drop out of school. Having a limited amount of education increases the likelihood that children in the foster care system may lead a life of homelessness.[63, 79] The current study attempted to gain insight into deficits in supports at home and at school that may contribute to the academic experience of foster care students. The findings of the current study coincided with the previous literature; participants made several references to students in the foster care system having several behavioral and emotional concerns as well as academic deficits. Specifically, participants stated that foster children are more withdrawn than the other students in the classroom and can become angry and combative. Academically, participants emphasized that many students in the foster care system have gaps in learning, but it becomes difficult to provide academic interventions to aid in closing the academic gaps.

According to Barnow et al., 2015, one of the reasons children in the foster care system experience difficulty in school is due to their instability prior to coming into foster care and the constant placement moves between foster homes. The lived experiences of the participants parallel these findings. School officials, who participated in the study, expressed that constant movements between placements cause children in the foster care system to become academically behind, and it also hinders any interventions that could possibly be implemented to aid the student's educational experience. Participants indicated that schools lack supplemental resources specifically geared towards children in the foster care system, or children with severe emotional and behavioral concerns. Resources of this nature, could prove beneficial in helping foster children become more academically successful.

Based on the finding of the research, another reason for the poor academic experiences of children in the foster care, which was the lack of training and preparation of teachers responsible for educating this population of students.[84] The current findings support the research that teachers, counselors, and administrators in Richmond County had not received appropriate training in working with foster children; unless they received it from an outside source. Because the needs of these children are vastly different from children who are not in the foster care system, it would be ineffective to treat them in the same manner. The behavior and emotional strains that foster children experience requires additional support that could be taught to school officials during professional learning opportunities.

IMPLICATIONS OF STUDY TO THEORETICAL FRAMEWORK

The main theory that provided the framework for the current study was Maslow's Hierarchy of Needs. According to the theory, individuals must begin at the bottom of the hierarchy and fulfill those needs before moving onto the next level. The hierarchy begins with the physiological needs of food, clothing, and shelter. Then moves to the next levels of security, love and belonging, and esteem; all contributing to the final stage of self-actualization.[88, 67]

It was proposed that children in the foster care system lack the basic physiological needs including food, clothing, and shelter due to their unfortunate circumstances. Based upon the basic principles of the theory, if the children in foster care are missing the most basic level of care, they will not be able to progress throughout the hierarchy. The inability to sufficiently satisfy basic needs, prohibits the individual of achieving safety, love and belong, esteem, and ultimately self-actualization. [88, 67] Without fulfilling each level of the hierarchy, it would be difficult for a child to maintain a positive academic experience.

However, the data of the current study showed foster parents are taking care of the basic needs for the foster children in their home. This indicates that the preliminary level in the hierarchy is being satisfied, but because of the behavioral and emotional concerns expressed by the participants, it suggests deficits in the latter levels of safety, love and belong, and esteem. Due to the traumatic circumstances foster children experience, that ultimately lead them into foster care, it is not outlandish to infer that foster children have issues with trust and building relationships. The inability of foster children to fill these deficits both independently or with assistance, negatively impacts their academic experiences and is reflected in the responses of the participants in the current study.

Supplemental theories were used to create the theoretical framework for the current study: Bowen family systems theory and Bowlby's Attachment theory. Bowen family systems theory focuses on the combination of emotional and relational systems that exist within a family.[64] Plainly stated, the emotional turmoil and stress that one family member is experiencing may be transmitted to other members in the family and could ultimately lead to negative behavior.[64, 66] Bowen's theory further explains that children who have experienced abuse by family members may engage in self-harm or disengage completely. These students may also experience anxiety and engage in delinquent behavior.[66] Based upon the responses of the participants regarding the emotional and behavioral concerns of children in the foster care system, it would appear that Bowen's family theory may provide an explanation for the observed behaviors. One of the ways children can enter foster care is due to physical abuse or neglect. If foster children have experienced abuse by the hands of their former caregiver, it may provide justification to the behaviors observed by the teachers, counselors, and administrators in the study. The responses regarding observed behaviors include: "traumatized," "impulsive," "rude," "withdrawn," and "angry".

Further, Bowlby's Attachment Theory focuses on the initial attachments children form with their first primary caregiver, which is normally identified as the mother. When something threatens that attachment, it can have a lasting negative effect on the relational development of the child. When children are removed from their primary caregiver, they may go through a period of separation anxiety.[12, 90] This theory was presented in the current study because the instability of the child's life and potential abuse or neglect experienced, causing entrance into foster care, may have caused the child to develop insecure attachments.[101] Insecurely attached children have difficulty forming relationships and may suffer from psychological stressors.[12, 101] Additionally, being removed from that caregiver may also foster separation anxiety within the child. Taking all factors into consideration, Bowlby's Attachment Theory may provide some insight into the emotional and behavioral issues experienced by the foster children referenced in this study. This theory may provide an explanation as to the withdrawn nature described by some of the participants as well as the anger and anxiety foster children exhibit.

STUDY LIMITATIONS

One of the major limitations in the current study is the number of participants who willingly completed the questionnaire, eliminating control over the number of participants in the study. While 45 potential participants completed the informed consent, only 24 participants actually completed the survey. Of those 24 participants, five were removed because they did not meet the specified criteria to participate in the study. Within the 19 participants, there was only one counselor and one administrator. This limitation did not allow for a great deal of information to be gathered from diverse school officials. The majority of the information provided was afforded by elementary school teachers, who may have a different outlook on the domestic and home support of children in the foster care system than the counselors and administrators who also work with this population of students. Another limitation of the current study was the researcher's inability to speak with the participants. The participants conveyed their personal experiences by completing a questionnaire. The researcher was unable to ask participants follow-up questions or for further elaboration on responses that presented with vague details. This limited the researcher's availability of information extracted from the textual data that was provided by each participant. Lastly, the participants in the study were only solicited from an elementary school population in Augusta, Richmond County. The findings are unable to be generalized to other populations because the responses from middle and high school teachers, counselors, and administrators from other school districts may be drastically different from those participants in the current study. Additionally, the demographics of foster students and academic services provide vary by school system; therefore, if the study was conducted in a different county, the results may not be the same.

RECOMMENDATIONS FOR LEADERSHIP

The purpose of the qualitative narrative was to explore the perceptions of elementary teachers, counselors, and administrators as it related to the domestic and academic supports of children in the foster care system and the influence it may have on academic experience. The aim was to find potential early interventions for children in the foster care system if it was identified that the lack of support from the home or school was negatively impacting academic experience. By addressing these concerns early on in the academic process, school officials may be able to avoid further academic struggles; thus, decreasing the chances of foster care students dropping out of school or being subjected to a future of homelessness.[63, 79] Based upon the findings of the current study, the following recommendations are offered to leadership and school officials regarding the academic experience of students in the foster care system.

1.   One of the major themes expressed is that foster chil-

dren display a plethora of emotional and behavioral concerns. These emotional and behavioral concerns affect how the students perform academically and interacting with peers. If leadership collaborated with the school counselors to construct a behavioral plan including consistent counseling and a disciplinary proposal, this may aid students in dealing with some of the emotional and behavioral issues they are experiencing. Support groups for children in the foster care system can be formed within schools or county wide to allow those students to share their experiences and feel supported by others who are experiencing similar issues.[32, 107] The groups should be facilitated by the school counselors to allow students to learn positive coping mechanism in a safe and supportive environment.

2. Because students in the foster care system are academically behind due to instability before entering foster care or the constant transitions once being instated in foster care, it would be beneficial for leadership to formulate additional tutoring or remediation programs to allow those students to bridge academic gaps.[79] In addition to tutoring and remediation programs, a Response to Intervention packet (RTI) should be expedited in case the student moves placements. This RTI packet will provide interventions to help students meet academic goals. This documentation remains in the student's permanent record and will follow the student in case the child moves. This will allow the subsequent schools to know what academic modifications and interventions were put in place for the student, so they are able to continue.

3. One of the major concerns regarding the academic struggles of foster care students is their instability and transient nature. The researcher recommends leadership firmly enforce the McKinney-Vento Act, allowing foster care students to remain in their current school. One of the weaknesses in the act is the loose interpretation regarding the responsibility of transportation.[53, 72] A recommendation for leadership would be to provide transportation for foster care students to their zoned or current school to alleviate the burden placed on the foster parent and allow the student to stay in his or her school.

4. In reference to the lack of communication between the foster parents and the school, the researcher recommends appointing a liaison between the two parties to bridge the communication gap. This individual could be the school social worker, parent facilitator, or counselor.

5. Lastly, the data demonstrates a need for teachers, counselors, and school administrators to obtain training in working with foster care students. Specifically, those students who have significant emotional, behavioral, and academic concerns. Professional development classes can be formulated to provide the necessary tools needed to create a nurturing academic environment and the most appropriate way to handle children in the custody of a foster caretaker.[6, 79] This training may assist in enhancing the academic experience for foster care students, thus eliminating some of the struggles faced by foster care students.

RECOMMENDATIONS FOR FUTURE RESEARCH
While the current study exuded a significant amount of meaningful data, the study was limited to the elementary teachers, counselors, and administrators in Augusta, Richmond County. The current study could be replicated in neighboring counties in Georgia to see if the results are similar. This study could also be replicated in a middle school or high school setting. It is recommended to soliciting counselors and school administrators to complete the survey in an effort to obtain diversity among participants.

Additionally, future research is recommended to examine the effects of implementing academic and behavioral interventions for children in the foster care system. If these interventions prove successful, then foster care students should receive fewer behavioral referrals and academic achievement should improve. Further, future research can examine the perceptions of the foster children regarding the support they receive from foster caregivers and school. This may provide some insight into what these students feel they need, but are not getting from their caregivers or schools.

SUMMARY AND CONCLUSION

The purpose of this qualitative narrative inquiry study was to explore how elementary school teachers, counselors, and administrators perceive the domestic and academic supports children in the foster care system receive, and the influence it may have on academic comic experience. The participants in the study were elementary teachers, counselors, and administrators in the Augusta, Richmond County school system. Based upon the narrative responses provided by participants, that data suggested that children in the foster care system receive some support in the home, but are in need of additional services in school. A thematic analysis was conducted and the six major themes that emerged were (1) basic needs met; (2) caring and responsive foster parents; (3) lack of communication; (4) behavior and emotional concerns; (5) lack of student services; and (6) training. Basic needs referred to the foster parent meeting the basic needs of students. Some participants stated that foster parents only did the bare minimum, while others indicated they treated the child as their own. The data showed a significant amount of participants had personal experiences with foster parents who were caring and responsive; however, there could be a breakdown in communication due to their inability to be physically present at the school. Behavior and emotional concerns pertained to the presenting issues of the foster children. Lack of student services refers to a limited amount of resources provided in schools to address the concerns of this unique population of students, and training references the need for additional training for school officials working with children in the foster care system.

The results of the current study added to the limited body of literature regarding factors that hinder the academic progress of foster care students. This study also presented with several recommendations that could be potentially implemented to help alleviate some of the problems foster care students face, thus providing these students with a more positive outcome. The major theoretical backing for this study was Maslow's Hierarchy of Needs indicating that students in the foster care system lack many of the preliminary levels in the hierarchy contributing to a poor academic experience. While the data suggested that foster care children are getting basic needs met by foster parents, they have deficits in the areas of love and belonging and security. This is made evident by the emotional and behavioral concerns displayed by foster children.

The current study highlighted areas of improvement for elementary schools in Augusta, Richmond County that could be made to benefit children in the foster care system. The study also offers recommendations that could be implemented in the school system to alleviate some of the hardships experienced by foster care students. If interventions or improvement action plans are not implemented with fidelity, the future of children in the foster care system could lend itself to limited education or a life of homelessness.[63, 79]

REFERENCES

1. Ahmed, S. (2013). A Quality Analysis of Lean Six Sigma and the Effects on the Management Firm. Journal of American Academy of Business, Cambridge, 18(2), 291-296. Retrieved from http://www.jaabc.com

2. Akin, B. A. (2011). Predictors of foster care exits to permanency: A competing risks analysis of reunification, guardianship, or adoption. Children and Youth Services Review, 33, 999-1011. Retrieved from http://ac.els-cdn.com.contentproxy.phoenix.edu/S0190740911000193/1-s2.0-S0190740911000193-main.pdf?_tid=7b72c3e2-66a8-11e7-b3a1-00000aacb35e&acdnat=1499826127_4d13ddeac7db-1b4496ee134a7bec5c15

3. Barnow, B. S., Buck, A., O'Brien, K., Pecora, P., Ellis, M. L., & Steiner, E. (2015). Effective services for improving education and employment outcomes for children and alumni of foster care service: Correlates and educational and employment outcomes. Child & Family Social Work, 20(2), 159-170. doi:10.1111/cfs.12063

4. Bernedo, I. M., Salas, M. D., García-Martín, M. A., & Fuentes, M. J. (2012). Teacher assessment of behavior problems in foster care children. Children and Youth Services Review, 34(4), 615-621. doi:10.1016/j.childyouth.2011.12.003

5. Benson, P. (2014). Narrative Inquiry in Applied Linguistics Research. Annual Review of Applied Linguistics, 34(1), 154-170.

6. Birneanu, A. (2013). Behavior problems in foster care children. Revista de AsistentaSociala. 12(4), 14-23. Retrieved

from http://web.b.ebscohost.com.contentproxy.

7. phoenix.edu/ehost/pdfviewer/pdfviewer?vid=6&sid=074032e 8-b254-4c88-89ca-a564a1238de4%40sessionmgr120&hid=102

8. Bold, C. (2012). Collecting narrative data. London: SAGE Publications Ltd. doi:10.4135/9781446288160.n6

9. Booth, J., & Nelson, A. (2013). Sharing stories: Using narratives to illustrate the role of critical reflection in practice with first Australians. Occupational Therapy International, 20(3), 114-123. doi:10.1002/oti.1343

10. Braun, V., & Clarke, V. (2006). Using thematic analysis in psychology. Qualitative Research in Psychology, 3(2), 77-101. doi:http://dx.doi.org.contentproxy.phoenix.edu

11. /10.1191/1478088706qp063oa

12. Bretherton, I. (1992). The origins of attachment theory: John Bowlby and Mary Ainsworth. Developmental Psychology, 28, 759-775.

13. Brown, J. D. (2008). Foster parents' perceptions of factors needed for successful foster placements. Journal of Child and Family Studies, 17, 538–554. doi:10.1007/s10826-007-9172-z

14. Brown, J. D., & Bednar, L. M. (2006). Foster parent perceptions of placement breakdown. Children and Youth Services Review, 28(12), 1497-1511. doi:10.1016/j.childyouth.2006.03.004

15. Brown, J. D., & Campbell, M. (2007). Foster parent perceptions of placement success. Children and Youth Services Review, 29, 1010–1020. doi:10.1016/j.childyouth.2007.02.002

16. Chamberlain, P., Price, J. M., Reid, J. B., Landsverk, J., Fisher, P. A., & Stoolmiller, M. (2006). Who disrupts from

placement in foster and kinship care? Child Abuse & Neglect, 30(4), 409-424. doi:10.1016/j.chiabu.2005.11.004

17. Chambers, R. M., Crutchfield, R. M., Willis, T. Y., Cuza, H. A., Otero, A., & Carmichael, H. (2017). Perspectives: Former foster youth refining the definition of placement moves. Children and Youth Services Review, 73, 392-397. doi:10.1016/j.childyouth.2017.01.010

18. Chambers-Nash, C. J. (2013). A case study of education support and services for foster children.

19. (Doctoral dissertation). Available from ProQuest Dissertations & Theses database. (UMI No. 3570367)

20. Chambers, C., & Palmer, E. (2011). Educational stability for children in foster care. Touro Law Review, 26(4), 1103.

21. Chenail, R. J. (2011). Interviewing the investigator: Strategies for addressing instrumentation and researcher bias concerns in qualitative research. The Qualitative Report, 16(1), 255-262. Retrieved from https://search.proquest.com/docview/854984835?accountid=458

22. Cheung, C., Lwin, K., & Jenkins, J. M. (2012). Helping youth in care succeed: Influence of caregiver involvement on academic achievement. Children and Youth Services Review, 34(6), 1092-1100. doi:10.1016/j.childyouth.2012.01.033

23. Christian, S. (2003). Educating children in foster care. National Conference of State Legislators, 1-19. Retrieved from https://www.ncsl.org/print/cyf/foster_care_education.pdf

24. Clandinin, D. J., & Connelly, F. M. (2000). Narrative inquiry: Experience and story in qualitative research. San Francisco: Jossey-Bass.

25. Clandinin, D. J. (2006). Narrative inquiry: A methodology

for studying lived experience. Research Studies in Music Education, 27(1), 44-54. doi: 10.1177/1321103X060270010301

26. Cleary, M., Horsfall, J., & Hayter, M. (2014). Data collection and sampling in qualitative research: does size matter? Journal of Advanced Nursing, 70(3), 473-475 3p. doi:10.1111/jan.12163

27. Connelly, F.M., & Clandinin, D.J. (1990). Stories of Experience and Narrative Inquiry. Educational Researcher, 19(5), 2-14.

28. Connelly, L. M. (2014). Understanding case studies. MED-SURG Nursing, 23(6), 422-424. Retrieved from://search.ebscohost.com.contentproxy.phoenix.edu/login.aspx? direct=true&db=ccm&AN=103925719&site=ehostlive

29. Connelly, L. M. (2016). Trustworthiness in qualitative research. Medsurg Nursing, 25(6), 435-436. Retrieved from https://search.proquest.com/docview/1849700459?accountid=458

30. Cooley, M. E., & Petren, R. E. (2011). Foster parent perceptions of competency: Implications for foster parent training. Children and Youth Services Review, 33(10), 1968-1974. doi:10.1016/j.childyouth.2011.05.023

31. Cope, D. G. (2014). Methods and meanings: Credibility and trustworthiness of qualitative research. Oncology Nursing Forum, 41(1), 89-91. Retrieved from https://search.proquest.com/docview/1476482511?accountid=458

32. Cox, T. L. (2013). Improving educational outcomes for children and youth in foster care. Children and Schools, 35(1), 59-62. doi:10.1093/cs/cds040

33. Creswell, J. W. (1995). Educational research: Planning, conducting, and evaluating quantitative and qualitative

research. Columbus, OH: Merrill/Prentice Hall.

34. Creswell, J. W. (1998). Qualitative inquiry and research design: Choosing among five traditions. Thousand Oaks, CA: Sage Publications.

35. Creswell, J. W. (2013). Qualitative inquiry and research design: Choosing among five approaches (3rd ed.). Thousand Oaks, CA: Sage Publications

36. Creswell, J. W. (2014). Research design: Qualitative, quantitative, and mixed methods approaches (4th ed.). Thousand Oaks, CA: Sage Publications.

37. Drazen, J. M., Harrington, D. P., McMurray, J. V., Ware, J. H., Woodcock, J., Grady, C., Kang, G. (2017). The changing face of clinical trials: Informed consent. The New England Journal of Medicine, 376(9), 856-867. Retrieved from https://search.proquest.com/docview/1873745603?accountid=458

38. Dworkin, S. (2012). Sample Size Policy for Qualitative Studies Using In-Depth Interviews. Archives of Sexual Behavior. pp. 1319-1320. doi:10.1007/s10508-012-0016-6

39. Evans, L. D. (2004). Academic achievement of students in foster care: Impeded or improved? Psychology in the Schools, 41(5), 527-535. doi:10.1002/pits.10179

40. Evans, R., Hallett, S., Reese, A., & Roberts, L. (2016). The acceptability of educational interventions: Qualitative evidence from children and young people in care. Children and Youth Services Review, 71, 68-76. doi: 10.1016/j.childyouth.2016.10.030

41. FindLaw. (2013). Foster care: Background and history. Retrieved from http://files.findlaw.com/pdf/family/family.findlaw.com_foster-care_foster-care-background-and-histo-

ry.pdf

42. Flynn, R. J., Marquis, R. A., Paquet, M., Peeke, L. M., & Aubry, T. D. (2012). Effects of individual direct-instruction tutoring on foster children's academic skills: A randomized trial. Children and Youth Services Review, 34(6), 1183-1189. doi:10.1016/j.childyouth.2012.01.036

43. Font, S. A. (2014). Kinship and nonrelative foster care: The effect of placement type on child Well-Being. Child Development, 85(5), 2074-2090. doi:10.1111/cdev.12241

44. Forsman, H., Vinnerljung, B. (2012). Interventions aiming to improve school achievements of children in out-of-home care: A scoping review. Children and Youth Services Review, 34(6), 1084-1091. doi:10.1016/j.childyouth.2012.01.037

45. Fusch, P. I., & Ness, L. R. (2015). Are we there yet? Data saturation in qualitative research. The Qualitative Report, 20(9), 1408-1416. Retrieved from https://search.proquest.com/docview/1721368991?accountid=458

46. Georgia Division of Family and Children Services. (2016). Foster Care and Adoptions. Retrieved from http://dfcs.dhs.georgia.gov/sites/dfcs.dhs.georgia.gov /files/Adoptions%20 Page%20-%202016.pdf

47. Gonzalez, E.T. (2000). Cognitive and behavioral/emotional development of Latino children in foster care. Dissertation Abstracts International: Section B: The Sciences and Engineering, 60–9B, 4888.

48. Goodyer, A. (2016). Children's accounts of moving to a foster home. Child & Family Social Work, 21(2), 188-197. doi:10.1111/cfs.12128

49. Goulding, C. (2005). Grounded theory: Ethnography and phenomenology. European Journal of Marketing, 39(3/4),

294-308.

50. Gowan, B. G. M. (2005). Historical evolution of child welfare services. Child Welfare for the Twenty-first Century: A Handbook of Practices, Policies, & Programs, 10-40.

51. Green, H. E. (2014). Use of theoretical and conceptual frameworks in qualitative research. Nurse Researcher, 21(6), 34-38. doi:10.7748/nr.21.6.34.e1252

52. Greeno, E. J., Lee, B. R., Uretsky, M. C., Moore, J. E., Barth, R. P., & Shaw, T. V. (2016). Effects of a foster parent training intervention on child behavior, caregiver stress, and parenting style. Journal of Child and Family Studioes, 25(6), 1991-2000. doi:http://dx.doi.org/10.1007/s10826-015-0357-6

53. Hernandez Jozefowicz-Simbeni, D. M., & Israel, N. (2006). Services to homeless students and families: The McKinney-vento act and its implications for school social work practice. Children & Schools, 28(1), 37-44. Retrieved from https://search.proquest.com/docview/210929284?accountid=458

54. Hope, C. J., Hornung Garvin, J., & Sauer, B. C. (2012). Information extraction from narrative data. American Journal of Health-System Pharmacy, 69(6), 455-461. doi:10.2146/ajhp110135

55. IRBNet.org. (2017). IRB guidance- pilot studies, field test and the IRB review. Retrieved from htttps://www.irbnet.org/release/projects.do

56. Jack, B. (2010). Giving them a voice: the value of qualitative research. Nurse Researcher, 17(3), 4-6. Retrieved from http://search.ebscohost.com.contentproxy.phoenix.edu/login.aspx? direct=true&db=ccm&AN=105185215&site=ehostlive

57. Jalongo, M. R. (2006). The story of Mary Ellen Wilson: Tracing the origins of child protection in America. Early Childhood Education Journal, 34(1), 1-4.

58. James, S. (2004). Why do foster care placements disrupt? An investigation of reasons for placement change in foster care. Social Service Review, 78(4), 601-627.

59. Joyce, M. (2015). Using narrative in nursing research. Nursing Standard Royal College of Nursing 29(38), 36. doi:10.7748/ns.29.38.36.e9008

60. Katz, M. B. (1996). In the shadow of the poorhouse: A social history of welfare in America. New York, NY: Perseus Basic Books.

61. Keller, E., Wetherbee, K., Le Prohn, S., Payne, V., Sim, K., & Lamont, R. (2001). Competencies and problems behavior of children in family foster care: Variations by kinship placement status and race. Children and Youth Services Review, 23(12), 915–940.

62. Kirk, C. M., Lewis, R. K., Nilsen, C., & Colvin, D. Q. (2013). Foster care and college: The educational aspirations and expectations of youth in the foster care system. Youth & Society, 45(3), 307-323. doi:10.1177/0044118X11417734

63. Kishore, A. R., & Shaji, K. S. (2012). School Dropouts: Examining the Space of Reasons. Indian Journal of Psychological Medicine, 34(4), 318-323. doi:10.4103/0253-7176.108201

64. Knauth, D. G. (2003). Family secrets: An illustrative clinical case study guided by Bowen family systems theory. Journal of Family Nursing, 9(3), 331-33. doi:10.1177/1074840703255451

65. Kolbert, J. B., Crothers, L. M., Field, J. E. (2013). Clinical interventions with adolescents using a family systems approach. The Family Journal: Counseling

and Therapy for Couples and Families, 2(1), 87-94. doi:10.1177/1066480712456826

66. MacKay, L. (2012). Trauma and Bowen family systems theory: Working with adults who were abused as children. The Australian and New Zealand Journal of Family Therapy 33(3), 232-241. doi:10.1017/aft.2012.28

67. Maslow, A. H. (1943). A theory of human motivation. Psychological Review, 50, 370-396. Merriam-Webster's collegiate dictionary (10th ed.). (1993). Springfield, MA: Merriam-Webster

68. Mathes, E. W. (1981). Maslow's hierarchy of needs as a guide for living. Journal of Humanistic Psychology, 21(4), 69-72.

69. McLeod, S. (2007). Maslow's hierarchy of needs. Simply Psychology, 1.

70. Meese, R. L. (2012). MODERN FAMILY: Adoption and foster care in children's literature. The Reading Teacher, 66(2), 129-137. doi:10.1002/TRTR.01112

71. Merriam, S. B., & Tisdell, E. J. (2016). Qualitative research: A guide to design and implementation. (4th ed.). San Francisco: Wiley & Sons

72. Miller, P. M. (2011). An examination of the McKinney-vento act and its influence on the homeless education situation. Educational Policy, 25(3), 424-450. doi:10.1177/0895904809351692

73. Miller, J. J., & Collins-Camargo, C. (2016). Success on their own terms: Youths' perspectives on successful foster care. Journal of Public Child Welfare, 10(1), 59. doi:10.1080/155487 32.2015.1089813

74. Morton, B. (2015). Seeking safety, finding abuse: Stories

from foster youth on maltreatment and its impact on academic achievement. Child & Youth Services, 36(3), 205-225. doi:10.1080/0145935X.2015.1037047

75. Morton, B. M. (2016). The power of community: How foster parents, teachers, and community members support academic achievement for foster youth. Journal of Research in Childhood Education, 30(1), 99. doi:10.1080/02568543.2015.1105334

76. Moustakas, C. (1994). Phenomenological research methods. Thousand Oaks, CA: Sage.

77.

78. Nasir, M., Khalid, A., & Shoukat, A. (2014). Maslow theory of human development and emergence of street children phenomenon in Pakistan. Pakistan Vision, 15(2), 98-123.

79. Neely, P., & Griffin-Williams, A. (2013). High school dropouts contribute to juvenile delinquency. Review of Higher Education and Self-Learning, 6(22), 66-72. Retrieved from http://web.a.ebscohost.com.contentproxy.phoenix.edu/ehost/pdfviewer/ pdfviewer?sid=c42a3817-7601-4121-a1fo 13c911d3a1a7%40sessionmgr 4001&vid=35&hid=4214

80. Palinkas, L. A., Horwitz, S. M., Green, C. A., Wisdom, J. P., Duan, N., & Hoagwood, K. (2015). Purposeful sampling for qualitative data collection and analysis in mixed method implementation research. Administration and Policy in Mental Health and Mental Health Services Research, 42(5), 533-544. doi:http://dx.doi.org/10.1007/s10488-013-0528-y

81. Peters, K., & Halcomb, E. (2015). Interviews in qualitative research. Nurse Research, 22(4), 6. doi:http://dx.doi.org/10.7748/nr.22.4.6.s2

82. Price, J. M., Chamberlain, P., Landsverk, J., Reid, J. B.,

Leve, L. D., & Laurent, H. (2008). Effects of a foster parent training intervention on placement changes of children in foster care. Child Maltreatment, 13(1), 64-75. doi:10.1177/1077559507310612

83. Riessman, C. K. (2008). Narrative methods for the human sciences. Thousand Oaks, CA: Sage.

84. Rios, S. J., & Rocco, T. S. (2014). From foster care to college: Barriers and supports on the road to postsecondary education. Emerging Adulthood, 2(3), 227-237. doi: 10.1177/2167696814526715

85. Roberts, P., Priest, H., & Traynor, M. (2006). Reliability and validity in research. Nursing Standard, 20(44), 41-45. Retrieved from http://web.b.ebscohost.com. contentproxy.phoenix.edu/ehost/pdfviewer/pdfviewer?vid=9&sid=2e3f93fb-15e7-4cb4-af26-d6be680fadac%40sessionmgr106&hid=109

86. Rooij, v., F, Maaskant, A., Weijers, I., Weijers, D., & Hermanns, J. (2015). Planned and unplanned terminations of foster care placements in the Netherlands: Relationships with characteristics of foster children and foster placements. Children and Youth Services Review, 53, 130-136. doi:10.1016/j.childyouth.2015.03.022

87. Russell, J., & Summers, A. (2013). Reflective decision-making and foster care placements. Psychology, Public Policy, and Law, 19(2), 127-136. doi:http://dx.doi.org/10.1037/a0031582

88. Salas, M. M., García-Martín, M., Fuentes, M., &Bernedo, I. (2015). Children's emotional and behavioral problems in the foster family context. Journal of Child & Family Studies, 24(5), 1373-1383. doi:10.1007/s10826-014-9944-1

89. Scherr, T. G. (2007). Educational experiences of children in

foster care: Meta-analyses of special education, retention and discipline rates. School Psychology International, 28(4), 419-436. doi:10.1177/0143034307084133

90. Schwartz, J. (2015). The unacknowledged history of John Bowlby's attachment theory. British Journal of Psychotherapy, 31(2), 251-266. doi:10.1111/bjp.12149

91. Simms, M.D. (1991). Foster children and the foster care system. Part II: Impact on the child. Current Problems in Pediatrics, 21, 345–369.

92. Stevenson-Hinde, J. (2007). Attachment theory and John Bowlby: Some reflections. Attachment & Human Development, 9(4), 337-342. doi:10.1080/14616730701711540

93. Thomas, S. (2012) Narrative inquiry: Embracing the possibilities. Qualitative Research Journal, 12(2), 206-221. doi:10.1108/14439881211248356

94. Tobin, G., & Begley, C. (2004). Methodological rigor within a qualitative framework. Journal of Advanced Nursing, 48(4), 388-396 9p. doi:10.1111/j.1365-2648.2004.03207.x

95. Trattner, W. I. (2007). From poor law to welfare state: A history of social welfare in America. Simon and Schuster.

96. Tyler, K. A., & Melander, L. A. (2010). Foster care placement, poor parenting, and negative outcomes among homeless young adults. Journal of Child and Family Studies, 19(6), 787-794. doi:http://dx.doi.org/10.1007/s10826-010-9370-y

97. Tyre, A. (2012). Educational supports for middle school youth involved in the foster care system. Children and Schools, 34(4), 231-238. Retrieved from http://web.a.ebscohost.com. contentproxy.phoenix.edu/ehost/pdfviewer / pdfviewer?sid=c42a3817-7601-4121-a1f0-13c911d3a1a7%40sessionmgr4001&vid=41&hid=4214

98. U.S. Department of Health and Human Services, Administration for Children and Families, Administration on Children, Youth and Families, Children's Bureau. (2016). Afcars Report. Retrieved from http://www.acf.hhs.gov/programs/cb

99. U.S. Department of Health and Human Services. (2017). Information on protection of human subjects in research funded or regulated by U.S. government. Retrieved from https://www.hhs.gov/1946inoculationstudy/protection.html

100. Vacca, J. S. (2008). Breaking the cycle of academic failure for foster children — what can the schools do to help? Children and Youth Services Review, 30(9), 1081-1087. doi:10.1016/j.childyouth.2008.02.003

101. Vicedo, M. (2011). The social nature of the mother's tie to her child: John Bowlby's theory of attachment in post-war America. British Journal for the History of Science, 44(3), 401-426. doi:http://dx.doi.org/10.1017/S0007087411000318

102. Waid, J., Kothari, B. H., Bank, L., & McBeath, B. (2016). Foster care placement change: The role of family dynamics and household composition. Children and Youth Services Review, 68, 44-50. doi:10.1016/j.childyouth.2016.06.024

103. Ward, H. (2009). Patterns of instability: Moves within the care system, their reasons, contexts and consequences. Children and Youth Services Review, 31(10), 1113-1118. doi:10.1016/j.childyouth.2009.07.009

104. Yin, R. K. (2014). Case study research design and methods (5th ed.). Thousand Oaks, CA: Sage.

105. Zamawe, F. C. (2015). The implication of using NVivo software in qualitative data analysis: evidence-based reflections. Malawi Medical Journal: The Journal of Medical Association of Malawi, 27(1), 13-15. Retrieved from http://

search.ebscohost.com.contentproxy.phoenix.edu/ login.aspx?
direct=true&db=mdc&AN=26137192&site=ehostlive

106. Zetlin, A. G., Weinberg, L. A., & Shea, N. M. (2006).
Improving educational prospects for youth in foster care:
The education liaison model. Intervention in School &
Clinic, 41.5 267. Retrieved from bhttp://www.questia.com/
PM.qst?a=o&d=5014897982N

107. Zetlin, A., Weinberg, L., &Shea, N. M. (2010). Caregivers,
School Liaisons, and Agency Advocates speak out about the
educational needs of children and youths in foster care. Social Work, 55(3), 245-254. doi: 10.1093/sw/55.3.245

108. Zima, B. T., Bussing, R., Freeman, X. Y., & al, e. (2000).
Behavior problems, academic skill delays and school
failure among school-aged children in foster care: Their
relationship to placement characteristics. Journal of
Child and Family Studies, 9(1), 87-103. doi:http://dx.doi.
org/10.1023/A:1009415800475

About The Author

Dr. Brittany Ashton Bush is a native of Augusta, GA where she attended Davidson Fine Arts for middle and high school. Following graduation in 2005, Brittany attended North Carolina A & T, then later transferred to Georgia Southern University where she earned a degree in psychology and early childhood education. Following her undergraduate career, Brittany attended Augusta State University and obtained a Master's degree in clinical/counseling psychology, as well as a Master of Arts in Teaching. Moreover, Brittany completed her doctoral degree in Educational Leadership from the University of Phoenix.

Aside from her scholastic endeavors, Dr. Bush is employed with the Richmond County Board of Education as an early intervention reading teacher for kindergarten-5th grade students. Previously, Dr. Bush was a fifth grade English Language Arts and science teacher. While holding this position, Dr. Bush organized and directed the first dance team at her elementary school. She also founded a mentoring program for 5th grade boys; where she collaborated with the Men's basketball team at Augusta University to serve as mentors for her Jocks and Gents Mentoring Program. Dr. Bush won Teacher of the Year for the 2017-2018 school year, as well as the Governor's Greatest Gaines Award in 2016 and 2017 for the academic achievements of her 5th grade students on the Georgia Milestone Test. Before becoming an educator Dr. Bush served as a child advocate for children in the foster care system. She advocated for the best interests of those children both personally and academically.

Additionally, Dr. Bush is an adjunct professor at Aiken Technical College in the Early Childhood Department. She was the recipient of Child Enrichment's Ambassador Award in 2017 for her "unwavering dedication to children and support for Child Enrichment". She was also recognized by Women Who Work as a 2017 recipient of the Honorable 20 in the fields of education and mentorship. Further, Dr. Bush was recognized by the Augusta Chamber of Commerce as one of Augusta's Top 10 Young Professionals to Watch in 2018.

To contact the author, send inquiries and requests to:

Email: BrittanyBush319@yahoo.com
Instagram: Inspiration319

CPSIA information can be obtained
at www.ICGtesting.com
Printed in the USA
FSHW010853050320
67668FS